The Happy Princess

Nicholas Allan

RED FOX

To Amanda and Steve

A Red Fox Book

Published by Random House Children's Books
20 Vauxhall Bridge Road, London SW1V 2SA

A division of Random House UK Ltd
London Melbourne Sydney Auckland
Johannesburg and agencies throughout the world

1 3 5 7 9 10 8 6 4 2

First published simultaneously in hardback and paperback by
Hutchinson Children's Books and Red Fox 1997

Printed and bound in Belgium by
Proost International Book Production

RANDOM HOUSE UK Limited Reg. No. 954009

ISBN 0 09 926475 7

Diana was a happy baby.

When she was a little girl
she was brilliant at
swimming ...

... and dancing.

But she didn't think she was good at
anything else, especially sums ...

... and horse-riding.

But one thing Diana was <u>very</u> good at was
caring for people – just like Snow White.
So she got a job as a nanny.

But soon after that she was offered
a job as a princess.

The marriage was very important,
so she had to have an extra-long train.

It was a beautiful day for the wedding.
There were lots of people and carriages

(though Diana kept away from the horses).
She thought she could never be happier now she was a princess.

She met Elton John ...

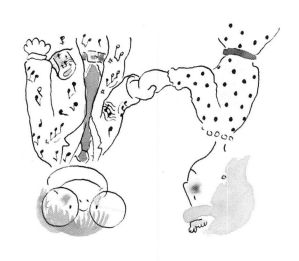

... and the President of the United States of America ...

... and she travelled all over the world.

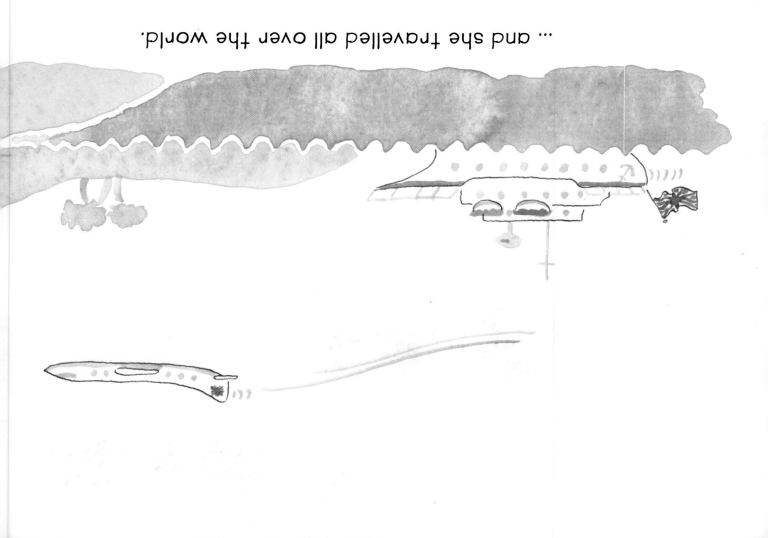

But being a princess wasn't always easy ...

... and sometimes Diana didn't say the right things.

Sometimes she didn't get on with the Queen ...

... or the Queen's horses.

And sometimes she was so lonely

she danced all by herself.

In the end she became
so unhappy she even
stopped eating her greens!

Then she became very tired.

Diana began to wish she could have her old job back.
But she couldn't.
She was a princess.

But then one day, she thought, <u>because</u> she was a princess,
she could care for lots and lots of people –
even more than she ever could before.
So that's exactly what she did.

She cared for the homeless.   She cared for the sick.

She cared for the hungry.

She cared for the elderly ...

... and most of all, she cared for the children.
And that's how, at last, Diana became
The Happy Princess.

But where is her happiness now?
Has it all disappeared?
Has it blown away forever?
No, it's still here ...

... and here ...

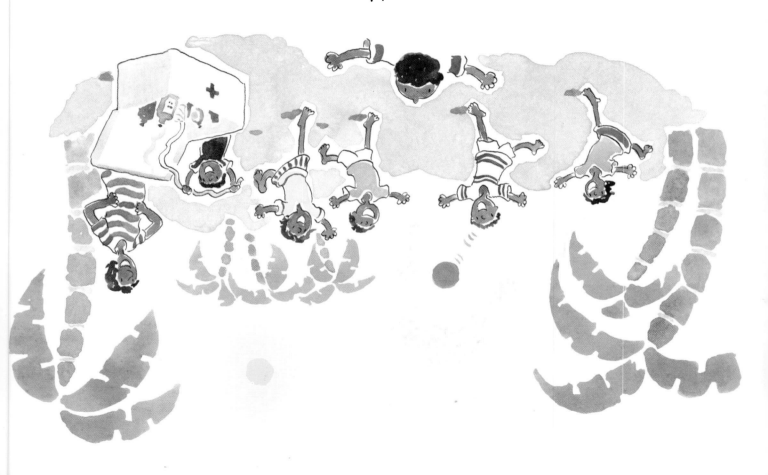

... and here, and probably ...

... even here.